The
Promise Land
Principle

Possessing God's Provisions
and Possibilities by Faith

RICHARD CHRISTENSON

authorHOUSE®

AuthorHouse™
1663 Liberty Drive
Bloomington, IN 47403
www.authorhouse.com
Phone: 1 (800) 839-8640

Published by AuthorHouse 09/14/2018

ISBN: 978-1-5462-6035-6 (sc)
ISBN: 978-1-5462-6034-9 (e)

Library of Congress Control Number: 2018910992

Print information available on the last page.

All of the Bible quotations used in the book are taken from the English Standard Version (ESV).

The Promise Land Principle is dedicated to those faithful followers of Jesus Christ who served together with me as God's "Foot of Faith" promise land missionaries at New Life Community Church in Elk Grove, California.

CONTENTS

INTRODUCTION

The book of Exodus provides us with one of the most dramatic adventures of faith found in the Bible. During its forty fantastic chapters we read about the enslavement of an entire race, a baby set afloat on the Nile River, a speaking shrub, a shepherd's staff becoming a venomous snake, water transformed into blood, miraculous frogs, gnats, flies, and locus infestations, a death angel, a sea selectively parting for the good guys and swallowing up the bad guys, a seemingly unlimited supply of flat bread on the ground in the desert every morning, birds dropping in for dinner, water flowing out of a rock, and much, much more. The stuff God pulls off in Exodus is way better than anything Indiana Jones, Iron Man, or even a Jedi relying upon the force could possibly accomplish. Seriously; someone should consider negotiating a film deal with God. I really believe the story that unfolds in Exodus would be a blockbuster success. Wait; has someone already done that movie?

As fun as it is to read this stupendous story, I want to make sure you don't miss the primary reason God inspired this book to be included in the Bible. This intriguing, inspirational narrative is about faith; how God goes about preparing His people to carry out their intended work and warfare with reliance upon His presence, power, and provision. The purpose and possibilities of our partnership with God are the primary teachings conveyed through all the awesome Exodus adventures.

Faith requires knowing with certainty what God has instructed us to do, and then doing it. Faith is always about compliance with God's commands and is intended to fill us with confidence; it is never based upon our best guess, good intentions, enlightened opinions, or flawed understanding.

"Faith is the assurance of things hoped for, the conviction of things not seen." **Hebrews 12:1**

Every follower of Christ was saved by faith. "For by grace you have been saved through faith. And this is not your own doing; it is the gift of God, not a result of works, so that no one may boast." **Ephesians 2:8, 9**

Subsequently, it is God's intent that followers of Christ fulfill our intended functions here on earth by faith. "The righteous shall live by faith." **Romans 1:17**

In order to function by faith, one of three things must be true.

1   We must take action based upon a promise God has recorded for us in the Bible.
2   We must put into practice a biblical principal that is properly understood, and appropriately applied.
3   We must take action based upon God's personal prompting.

As each episode in the Exodus story unfolds we find God preparing the faith that His people will require in order to accomplish His purpose and future plans. As we follow the journey of the Israelites from Egypt to Canaan we learn of the delays and disasters that always occur when we make the detrimental decision to do what we believe to be best rather than aligning our actions by faith with God's travel plans and timetable. Additionally, we will be given the opportunity to calculate the cost that inevitably comes from choosing to respond to the obstacles and opposition we encounter in fear rather than by faith.

I believe that God has a promise land He is offering to provide individually for every follower of Christ and corporately for every local church and Christian organization. Our choices concerning "The Promise Land Principle" will determine whether we end up prospering in our promise land or wandering in some wilderness.

Family Feud

The scenario that resulted in the Israelites relocating from their promise land in Canaan into enslavement in Egypt begins in Genesis 37. This sad story starts with the description of a dysfunctional family comprised of Jacob and his twelve sons. Although he was the father of eleven other boys, Jacob seemed to have a parental preference for his second-youngest son, Joseph. Their father's favoritism fostered intense hatred of Joseph by his ten older brothers.

To make matters worse, Jacob showcased his special love for Joseph by giving him a slick jacket. This gift only served to fuel the fire of resentment for Joseph by his siblings.

"When his brothers saw that their father loved him more than all his brothers, they hated him and could not speak peacefully to him." **Genesis 37:4**

Joseph's lack of tact and diplomacy during his adolescent years also contributed fuel to fire the family feud. Joseph had a strange dream which he proceeded to excitedly share with his jealous siblings illustrating what that famous philosopher Forest Gump once said, "Stupid is as stupid does."

"Now Joseph had a dream, and when he told it to his brothers they hated him even more. He said to them, 'Hear this dream that I have dreamed: Behold, we were binding sheaves in the field, and behold, my sheaf arose and stood upright. And behold, your sheaves gathered around it and bowed down to my sheaf.' His brothers said to him, 'Are you indeed to reign over us? Or are you indeed to rule over us?' So they hated him even more for his dreams and for his words." **Genesis 37:5-8**

Soon after that Joseph had a second dream that he couldn't wait to tell his unimpressed, and unappreciative brothers about.

"Then he dreamed another dream and told it to his brothers and said, 'Behold, I have dreamed another dream. Behold, the sun, the moon, and eleven stars were bowing down to me.'" **Genesis 37:9**

One day Joseph's brothers took their fathers flocks to graze at some pastures near Shechem. Soon after that Jacob sent Joseph to check up on them. When Joseph arrived at Shechem he learned that his brothers had moved the sheep to Dothan where he finally caught up with them.

When Joseph's brothers saw him coming decked out in his "In your face -- I'm dad's favorite" multi colored coat, they drafted a plan to immediately end his existence on earth.

"Come now, let us kill him and throw him into one of the pits. Then we will say that a fierce animal has devoured him, and we will see what will become of his dreams." **Genesis 37:20**

Fortunately for Joseph, his brother Reuben, the oldest of the bunch, intervened and persuaded the rest of these bad boys to adopt an alternative plan which involved selling their brother to some Midianite slave traders. After being sold, Joseph was taken to Egypt where he was auctioned off into slavery.

His brothers killed a goat and soaked Joseph's special coat in its blood. They then took the jacket to Jacob and suggested something bad may have happened to dad's cherished child; talk about cold!

"He identified it and said, 'It is my son's robe. A fierce animal has devoured him. Joseph is without doubt torn to pieces.' Then Jacob tore his garments and put sackcloth on his loins and mourned for his son many days. All his sons and all his daughters rose up to comfort him, but he refused to be comforted and said, 'No, I shall go down to Sheol to my son, mourning.' Thus his father wept for him." **Genesis 37:33-35**

Life Isn't Always Fair

Due to the jealousy of his brothers, Joseph was sold in slavery; How is that fair? The truth is, life isn't always fair for anyone, but through it all, God is always there. Nothing can happen to one of His children that our heavenly Father doesn't either plan or permit in accordance with the accomplishment of His purpose. What happened to Joseph was permitted because God had plans for him that required his relocation to Egypt.

"We know that for those who love God all things work together for good, for those who are called according to His purpose." **Romans 8:28**

After purchasing Joseph from his brothers, the Midianite slave traders took him to Egypt and sold him to a prominent Egyptian military officer named Potiphar.

"The LORD was with Joseph, and he became a successful man, and he was in the house of his Egyptian master. His master saw that the LORD was with him and that the LORD caused all that he did to succeed in his hands." **Genesis 39:2, 3**

Even in slavery, God ensured that whatever Joseph did was super successful. Every time life knocked him down, God caused him to bounce back up to a higher level of trust and responsibility according to His aims and agenda. Like the energizer rabbit, Joseph "took a lickin and kept right on tickin." He persevered by faith regardless of any and all seemingly unfair changes and challenges in his circumstances. That is how the faith of Christ's followers is intended to function whether life seems fair or unfair; regardless of our circumstances or the consequences of our choices or the choices of others.

Potiphar developed great admiration and respect for Joseph and as a result put him in charge of managing his entire estate; literally everything and everyone he owned. But God wasn't quite ready to end Joseph's story with; "He lived happily ever after." The fact is, his dramatic story was about to take another traumatic twist.

Apparently, Joseph was an extremely attractive young man, which did not go unnoticed by Potiphar's wicked wife. She made repeated attempts to seduce him, which initially he successfully ignored. He even attempted to reason with her.

"Because of me my master has no concern about anything in the house, and he has put everything that he has in my charge. He is not greater in this house than I am, nor has he kept back anything from me except you, because you are his wife. How then can I do this great wickedness and sin against God?" **Genesis 39:8, 9**

Talk about commendable conduct! This guy had real integrity. He did the right thing. I'm sad to say however, doing the right thing sometimes requires suffering and sacrifice.

One day Potiphar's persistent wife grabbed Joseph and insisted he have sexual relations with her. Joseph fled but she ripped his coat off of him as he attempted to escape and evade her seduction. Angered by his refusal to accommodate her, she started screaming and claiming Joseph had sexually assaulted her.

Unfortunately, when Potiphar heard his corrupt wife's contrived story, he believed her. Joseph was arrested and put in prison. Did I mention that life isn't always fair, but God is always there?

"But the LORD was with Joseph and showed him steadfast love and gave him favor in the sight of the keeper of the prison. And the keeper of the prison put Joseph in charge of all the prisoners who were in the prison. Whatever was done there, he was the one who did it. The keeper of the prison paid no attention to anything that was in Joseph's charge, because the LORD was with him. And whatever he did, the LORD made it succeed."
Genesis 29:21-23

Joseph had committed no crime, yet found himself doing hard time. You and I realize he was right where God intended for him to be; right where God permitted him to be. Some might even say, right where God put him. Regardless of how he got there, Joseph's story was right on schedule according to God's purpose and plan for his life.

While in jail, two particularly significant prisoners were entrusted to Joseph's care by the captain of the guard; both had been previously employed by the king of Egypt who they had somehow displeased. One was an officer who served the king wine, and the other was the king's baker.

One night both of these jail birds had dreams which distressed them. When Joseph noticed their forlorn faces he asked what was wrong.

"They said to him, 'We have had dreams, and there is no one to interpret them.' And Joseph said to them, 'Do not interpretations belong to God? Please tell them to me.'" **Genesis 40:8**

Amazingly God had equipped Joseph with the ability to interpret dreams; how coincidental! Joseph is in a particular prison listening to these two particular people who both have problems God has equipped him to help resolve. I think we all understand that God scripted this particular scenario.

Joseph listens to both dreams and tells these two guys that he has good news for the wine guy and bad news for the baker. The wine guy will get his job back in three days, but the baker is going to lose his head that very same day.

The wine guy is elated of course; the baker, not so much. Immediately after delivering good news to the wine guy, Joseph asks him for a favor.

"Remember me, when it is well with you, and please do me the kindness to mention me to Pharaoh, and so get me out of this house. For I was indeed stolen out of the land of the Hebrews, and here also I have done nothing that they should put me into the pit." **Exodus 40:14, 15**

Everything happened exactly as Joseph had predicated, however the wine guy forgot all about Joseph's request and alas God's innocent yet incarcerated servant remained in prison for the next two years until he was needed to interpret another dream.

The king of Egypt's dream is the next one we encounter in Joseph's storyline; something really weird involving seven fat, beautiful cows coming up out of the Nile River to graze, followed by seven scrawny, ugly cows. The next night the king's dream cast of characters changed to seven stout heads of grain growing on one stalk that got eaten by seven starving heads of grain. I've never had those particular nightmares myself, but I get how those visions could be disturbing. To make matters worse, none of the king's advisors had a clue what his dreams might mean. Any guess as to who might be available to help?

There was Joseph, in the right place, at the right time again. Amazing how that happened. Joseph tells the king that his dreams indicate what will take place in that part of the world during the next fourteen years; seven plentiful and productive years would be followed by seven years of severe drought. After explaining the meaning of the dreams, Joseph recommended that the king choose someone with great wisdom to store up supplies during the good times so Egypt would be able to have what they needed during the bad times. Guess who got a "get out of jail free" card and landed that prodigious job.

"Then Pharaoh said to Joseph, 'Since God has shown you all this, there is none so discerning and wise as you are. You shall be over my house, and all my people shall order themselves as you command. Only as regards the throne will I be greater than you.'" **Genesis 41:39, 40**

Everything played out in the years that followed exactly as Joseph predicted it would. Drought came upon the Middle Eastern part of the world and people were starving everywhere except in Egypt where, under Joseph's leadership, they had properly prepared for those terrible times.

It is during this period of time that Joseph's story takes another strange twist. His ten older brothers take a trip from Canaan to Egypt for the purpose of purchasing supplies. Joseph immediately recognizes them, but they have absolutely no idea who he is. Joseph proceeds to accuse them of being spies. In order to prove that they are innocent of espionage, they are required to return to Canaan and bring back Joseph's younger brother Benjamin. Everyone is set free but Simeon who is required to remain a prisoner in Egypt until the other nine bad boys return with their younger brother.

When his sons return home, their father Jacob is reluctant to part with Benjamin but eventually relents. Joseph's brothers make another trip to Egypt, this time bringing Benjamin with them. When they arrive, Joseph reveals to them who he really is. This may have been where the phrase, "out of the frying pan and into the fire" came from. Joseph instructs his brothers to return to Canaan and this time bring back his father Jacob.

"Thus Israel settled in the land of Egypt, in the land of Goshen. And they gained possessions in it, and were fruitful and multiplied greatly. And Jacob lived in the land of Egypt seventeen years. So the days of Jacob, the years of his life, were 147 years. And when the time drew near that Israel (another name for Jacob) must die, he called his son Joseph and said to him, 'If now I have found favor in your sight, put your hand under my thigh and promise to deal kindly and truly with me. Do not bury me in Egypt, but let me lie with my fathers. Carry me out of Egypt and bury me in their burying place.' He answered, 'I will do as you have said.'" **Genesis 47:27-30**

And that is how the Israelites ended up in Egypt for the next 400+ years. Initially, because of Joseph, the Israelites were treated well by the Egyptians, but soon after the death of Joseph, their presence in Egypt began being viewed as a liability rather than an asset.

"Now there arose a new king over Egypt, who did not know Joseph. And he said to his people, 'Behold, the people of Israel are too many and too mighty for us. Come, let us deal shrewdly with them, lest they multiply, and, if war breaks out, they join our enemies and fight against us and escape from the land.' Therefore they set taskmasters over them to afflict them with heavy burdens. They built for Pharaoh store cities, Pithom and Raamses. But the more they were oppressed, the more they multiplied and the more they spread abroad. And the Egyptians were in dread of the people of Israel. So they ruthlessly made the people of Israel work as slaves, and made their lives bitter with hard service, in mortar and brick, and in all kinds of work in the field. In all their work they ruthlessly made them work as slaves." **Exodus 1:8-14**

Please Send Someone Else

As the book of Exodus begins, we learn that the people of God were enduring slavery in Egypt. Due to their prolific population production, the king of Egypt issued a murderous moratorium involving the birth of Hebrew babies.

"Then Pharaoh commanded all his people, 'Every son that is born to the Hebrews you shall cast into the Nile, but you shall let every daughter live.'"
Exodus 1:22

During this period of time the birth of Moses takes place. His mother Jochebed, instead of complying with the king's command, under the watchful eye of his sister Miriam, put Moses in a basket located in the tall grass near the bank of the Nile River. When the daughter of the king of Egypt came for her daily bath, she spotted the basket and saw the baby boy. She knew that he was a Hebrew child, however she decided to protect and provide for him rather than terminate him. At that point Miriam stepped out of hiding and asked her if she would consider hiring someone to help care for the child. Miriam got her mother a paid position as a nanny for her own child.

Moses, who shouldn't have survived, was raised in the king of Egypt's household.

"Pharaoh's daughter adopted him and brought him up as her own son. And Moses was instructed in all the wisdom of the Egyptians, and he was mighty in his words and deeds." **Acts 7:21, 22**

Eventually, Moses learned about his Hebrew heritage, most likely from his mother or sister. When he was forty years of age (**Acts 7:23**), he came upon a Hebrew worker being savagely beaten by his Egyptian supervisor.

"He looked this way and that, and seeing no one, he struck down the Egyptian and hid him in the sand." **Exodus 2:12**

Moses, after looking left and right, impulsively took matters into his own hands. Never once did He look up. Apparently, it never occurred to him to ask God what he should do about the sad situation involving Hebrew slavery. His willfulness, and anger issues at this point in his life resulted in him spending the next forty years in the wilderness. Impulsive, independent action has never worked out well for me either; how about you?

We remember that Jacob and his family left the promise land God had provided for them of their own initiative. Just because a choice seems expedient in the short term, does not necessarily mean that it will work out well in the long term; particularly if it takes us away from the place God put us. **Exodus 2:23** tells us that the Israelites were treated terribly by the Egyptians and continually cried out to God for deliverance. Eventually God decided the time had come for them to return to their promise land. It was time to have a recruitment talk with Moses.

By this time Moses was married, eighty years of age, and living in Midian. While at work one day caring for his father-in-law Jethro's flock of sheep he unexpectedly he came upon a bush that was brightly burning but did not appear to be consumed by the flames. Since that seemed strange, he decided to check it out. What happen next took him completely by surprise; as I expect it would you or I.

"When the Lord saw that he turned aside to see, God called to him out of the bush, 'Moses, Moses!' And he said, 'Here I am.' Then he said, 'Do not come near; take your sandals off your feet, for the place on which you are standing is holy ground.' And He said, 'I am the God of your father, the God of Abraham, the God of Isaac, and the God of Jacob.' And Moses hid his face, for he was afraid to look at God. Then the LORD said, 'I have surely seen the affliction of my people who are in Egypt and have heard their cry because of their taskmasters. I know their sufferings, and I have come down to deliver them out of the hand of the Egyptians and to bring them up out of that land to a good and broad land, a land flowing with milk and honey, to the place of the Canaanites, the Hittites, the Amorites, the Perizzites, the Hivites, and the Jebusites. And now, behold, the cry of the people of Israel has come to Me, and I have also seen the oppression with which the Egyptians oppress them. Come, I will send you to Pharaoh that you may bring My people, the children of Israel, out of Egypt.'" **Exodus 3:4-10**

Moses at age forty may have felt that he was the right guy for the assignment God spoke of. Moses at age eighty responded, "Who am I? You've got the wrong guy."

What God said next to Moses needs to be etched into the brain of every follower of Christ so that it might be the first thing that comes to mind when we encounter circumstances that seem impossible, and choices that seem impractical.

"He (God) said, 'But I will be with you.'" **Exodus 3:12**

Followers of Christ are not required to do anything "for God" but rather "with God." It is our partnership with God that makes the impossible, possible. **Matthew 19:26**

Moses, however, remained reluctant to do what God wanted him to; he had more than a few concerns such as: "If I come to the people of Israel and say to them, 'The God of your fathers has sent me to you,' and they ask me, 'What is His name?' what shall I say to them?'" **Exodus 2:13**

Let me state the obvious: God's answer is a little brief: "Say this to the people of Israel: 'I Am has sent you.'" **Verse 14**

I'm not at all sure God's answer was entirely satisfactory much less completely understood by Moses; or us for that matter. Is every reader of Exodus clear about what God had in mind by telling Moses to refer to Him in that manner? Was that His pen name, or a perhaps a nick name? I thought God's name was Yahweh, Elohim, or maybe even El Shaddai; not "I Am." Could this reference possibly carry the same significance as the words of Jesus, "I am the Alpha and the Omega, the first and the last, the beginning and the end." **Revelation 22:13**

"Moses, when they ask you, 'Who sent you', tell them: 'The One Who has always been, and will continue being Whoever He has always been and will ever need to be.'"

Moses quickly expressed another concern about what God wanted him to do. "But behold, they will not believe me or listen to my voice, for they will say, 'The LORD did not appear to you.'" **Exodus 4:1**

Evidently it was time for some faith training, followed by some formative faith assessment. God instructs Moses to throw his shepherds staff on the ground and amazingly, he immediately complies with God's command by faith; without even complaining. Instantly the staff became a venomous snake. I'm with Indiana Jones at this point; I hate snakes--the sight of a snake makes me shake. What God tells Moses to do next may actually have been a deal breaker for me. "Put out your hand and catch it by the tail." **Exodus 4:4**

"Wait; what? God are you aware that picking the snake up by the tail will leave the business end free?"

Even though he likely had some serious concerns about what God instructed him to do; Moses again complied by faith. He was actually acing God's pop quiz. As soon as he picked up the snake, it became a staff again.

God tells Moses that this demonstration of His possibility power was provided to help him understand how He was going to go about getting the Israelites, and for that matter the Egyptians, to believe him. "I Am" proceeds to reinforce what Moses learned during faith lesson one, by providing him with faith lesson two.

"Again, the LORD said to him, 'Put your hand inside your cloak.' And he put his hand inside his cloak, and when he took it out, behold, his hand was leprous like snow. Then God said, 'Put your hand back inside your cloak.' So he put his hand back inside his cloak, and when he took it out, behold, it was restored like the rest of his flesh." **Exodus 4:6, 7**

I like to ask the question of those in the congregation at various points in my sermon, when I want to make sure they understand (not necessarily agree with) what I have just said; "Get it?" If they "Get it" I expect them to acknowledge by responding, "Got it." I see one of those "Get it/Got it" episodes occurring here between God and Moses.

God gives Moses more instructions about what to do if the Israelites refused to believe that "I Am" sent him after seeing demonstrations of His miraculous power. "If they will not believe even these two signs or listen to your voice, you shall take some water from the Nile and pour it on the dry ground, and the water that you shall take from the Nile will become blood on the dry ground." **Exodus 4:9**

So now Moses is good to go; right? Wrong! "But Moses said to the LORD, 'Oh, my LORD, I am not eloquent, either in the past or since you have spoken to your servant, but I am slow of speech and of tongue.'" **Exodus 4:10**

Moses is talking with a speaking shrub. If God can use a bush (not George) to speak with Moses, it seems pretty probable He can use Moses, or any of us for that matter, to speak with whoever He wants. Moses is obviously trying to find any excuse that will work. You and I certainly don't offer God excuses when He talks with us about living and laboring by faith, do we? We always have reasons for our reluctance; good reasons.

God however, wasn't buying what Moses was selling. "Then the LORD said to him, 'Who has made man's mouth? Who makes him mute, or deaf, or seeing, or blind? Is it not I, the LORD? Now therefore go, and I will be with your mouth and teach you what you shall speak.'" **Exodus 4:11, 12**

Finally Moses, in desperation and out of excuses, cuts to the chase. "Please send someone else." **Verse 13** "Here am I, Lord; send Aaron. He is really good at public speaking."

"Then the anger of the LORD was kindled against Moses and He said, 'Is there not Aaron, your brother, the Levite? I know that he can speak well. Behold, he is coming out to meet you, and when he sees you, he will be glad in his heart. You shall speak to him and put the words in his mouth, and I will be with your mouth and with his mouth and will teach you both what to do. He shall speak for you to the people, and he shall be your mouth, and you shall be as God to him. And take in your hand this staff, with which you shall do the signs.'" **Exodus 4:14-17**

The Promise Land Principle
CHAPTER 4

Purposeful Plagues

After his Midian meeting with God at the burning bush conference center Moses, age 80, and his brother Aaron, age 83, hot foot it off to Egypt. When these two old dudes arrived things initially went better than they expected.

"Moses and Aaron went and gathered together all the elders of the people of Israel. Aaron spoke all the words that the LORD had spoken to Moses and did the signs in the sight of the people. And the people believed; and when they heard that the LORD had visited the people of Israel and that He had seen their affliction, they bowed their heads and worshiped." **Exodus 4:29-31**

Unfortunately things didn't go as well when they told Pharaoh what God required him to do. "But Pharaoh said, 'Who is the LORD, that I should obey His voice and let Israel go? I do not know the LORD, and moreover, I will not let Israel go.'" **Exodus 5:2**

Instead of being cooperative and compliant, Pharaoh responded by implementing some rather harsh employment policies.

"The same day Pharaoh commanded the taskmasters of the people and their foremen, 'You shall no longer give the people straw to make bricks, as in the past; let them go and gather straw for themselves. But the number of bricks that they made in the past you shall impose on them, you shall by no means reduce it, for they are idle. Therefore they cry, 'Let us go and offer sacrifice to our God.' Let heavier work be laid on the men that they may labor at it and pay no regard to lying words.'" **Exodus 5:6-9**

When the Hebrews asked Pharaoh why they were being beaten more frequently and not being given the straw they required to meet their daily brick quota, they were told: "You troublemakers seem to have too much discretionary time. The real reason you want to go with Moses is that you are lazy and worthless. Don't blame me for making your lives more miserable than they already were. That is on you!"

So how does faith handle the times when we do what God tells us to and our circumstances get worse rather than better?

"They met Moses and Aaron, who were waiting for them, as they came out from Pharaoh; and they said to them, 'The LORD look on you and judge, because you have made us stink in the sight of Pharaoh and his servants, and have put a sword in their hand to kill us.'" **Exodus 5:20, 21**

Wait a second; why are God's people blaming Moses and Aaron? It was God who put them up to this. The fact is, neither of them wanted to take on this assignment. Life was a lot less hectic in Midian hanging out with the sheep and doing shepherding stuff. How will the faith of Moses and Aaron handle such unfair treatment by the Hebrews?

"Then Moses turned to the LORD and said, 'O LORD, why have you done evil to this people? Why did you ever send me? For since I came to Pharaoh to speak in Your name, he has done evil to this people, and You have not delivered your people at all.'" Exodus 5:22, 23

Pharaoh blames the Israelites, the Israelites blame the leaders God sent to them, and Moses blames God; a somewhat familiar scenario that sounds a lot like what went down between Adam and God in the Garden of Eden. "The man said, 'The woman whom you gave to be with me, she gave me fruit of the tree, and I ate.'" Genesis 3:12

Do things like that ever happen to you; at home, or work, or church? Is that really how faith is intended to function? I certainly hope not. Why do you think God included so many faith failures in the Bible? Is He pointing out some potential problems with our faith?

It is at this point that God says to Moses, "The time has come to use some purposeful plagues to convince Pharaoh and the Egyptians to take Me seriously. They need to know Who I Am; Who they are dealing with."

Please read this next text from Exodus carefully and prayerfully. What God has to say is fundamental, and foundational to those learning to function by faith.

"God spoke to Moses and said to him 'I am the LORD. I appeared to Abraham, to Isaac, and to Jacob, as God Almighty, but by My name the LORD I did not make Myself known to them. I also established My covenant with them to give them the land of Canaan, the land in which they lived as sojourners. Moreover, I have heard the groaning of the people of Israel whom the Egyptians hold as slaves, and I have remembered My covenant. Say therefore to the people of Israel, I am the LORD, and I will bring you out from under the burdens of the Egyptians, and I will deliver you from slavery to them, and I will redeem you with an outstretched arm and with great acts of judgment. I will take you to be my people, and I will be your God, and you shall know that I am the LORD your God, Who has brought you out from under the burdens of the Egyptians. I will bring you into the land that I swore to give to Abraham, to Isaac, and to Jacob. I will give it to you for a possession. I am the LORD.'" **Exodus 6:2-8**

God wants those who love and serve Him, to believe and totally trust Him by faith, regardless of the constantly changing circumstances of life; regardless of the consequences that result from our compliance with His commands. Sometimes God's purpose and plan require sacrifice and suffering from His saints. Sometimes God's will and work require carrying a cross. "And he said to all, 'If anyone would come after me, let him deny himself and take up his cross daily and follow me.'" Luke 9:23

What Jesus requires of His followers, God the Father first required of Him.

"Therefore, since we are surrounded by so great a cloud of witnesses, let us also lay aside every weight, and sin which clings so closely, and let us run with endurance the race that is set before us, looking to Jesus, the founder and perfecter of our faith, who for the joy that was set before Him endured the cross, despising the shame, and is seated at the right hand of the throne of God. Consider Him who endured from sinners such hostility against Himself, so that you may not grow weary or fainthearted." **Hebrews 12:1-3**

At this point in the Exodus story, no one's faith seems to be functioning.

"Moses spoke thus to the people of Israel, but they did not listen to Moses, because of their broken spirit and harsh slavery. So the LORD said to Moses, 'Go in, tell Pharaoh king of Egypt to let the people of Israel go out of his land.' But Moses said to the LORD, 'Behold, the people of Israel have not listened to me. How then shall Pharaoh listen to me, for I am of uncircumcised lips?' But the LORD spoke to Moses and Aaron and gave them a charge about the people of Israel and about Pharaoh king of Egypt: to bring the people of Israel out of the land of Egypt." **Exodus 6:9-13**

Amazingly, at least to me, Moses and Aaron, are able to schedule another meeting with Pharaoh. This time, however, God and Moses had a few attention grabbing tricks up their sleeves.

"Moses and Aaron went to Pharaoh and did just as the LORD commanded. Aaron cast down his staff before Pharaoh and his servants, and it became a serpent. Then Pharaoh summoned the wise men and the sorcerers, and they, the magicians of Egypt, also did the same by their secret arts. For each man cast down his staff, and they became serpents. But Aaron's staff swallowed up their staffs. Still Pharaoh's heart was hardened, and he would not listen to them, as the LORD had said." **Exodus 7:10-13**

I must have missed that transforming sticks into snakes class at seminary. I could have really used something like that during my 30+ years of local church leadership. So now what? Moses and Aaron told Pharaoh to let God's people go, and again he said, "No!" Did I mention that God is really good at playing "Truth or Consequences?"

God told Moses that it was the habit of the Pharaoh to take an early morning walk by the Nile River. Moses is instructed to meet him by the edge of the river and deliver another of God's messages accompanied by an attention getting demonstration of God's power.

"Say to him, 'The LORD, the God of the Hebrews, sent me to you, saying, 'Let my people go, that they may serve me in the wilderness.' But so far, you have not obeyed.' Thus says the LORD, 'By this you shall know that I am the LORD: behold, with the staff that is in my hand I will strike the water that is in the Nile, and it shall turn into blood. The fish in the Nile shall die, and the Nile will stink, and the Egyptians will grow weary of drinking water from the Nile.' And the LORD said to Moses, 'Say to Aaron, take your staff and stretch out your hand over the waters of Egypt, over their rivers, their canals, and their ponds, and all their pools of water, so that they may become blood, and there shall be blood throughout all the land of Egypt, even in vessels of wood and in vessels of stone.' Moses and Aaron did as the LORD commanded. In the sight of Pharaoh and in the sight of his servants he lifted up the staff and struck the water in the Nile, and all the water in the Nile turned into blood. And the fish in the Nile died, and the Nile stank, so that the Egyptians could not drink water from the Nile. There was blood throughout all the land of Egypt." Exodus 7:16-21

How did Pharaoh respond? He went back to his palace and attempted to ignore God's demands. When it comes to God, the word ignore always grows to become ignorance.

God responded to Pharaoh's refusal to hear and heed His demand by afflicting Egypt with a series of plagues whose purpose was intended to bring about Egypt's compliance with His commands.

Exodus Chapter 8   Frogs, gnats, and flies selectively filled the land of Egypt except for the region of Goshen where the Hebrews lived.

Exodus Chapter 9   All the Egyptian's animals contracted some terrible disease. The entire population of Egypt was afflicted with boils and skin sores, and the worst hailstorm the country had ever experienced fell everywhere except Goshen.

Exodus Chapter 10   More locusts than anyone had ever seen before arrived and ate every growing thing in Egypt. Meanwhile, Pharaoh attempted to con God's guys. He promised to do what God wanted if the plagues stopped. God agreed and honored His side of the contract, as He always does, however, Pharaoh did not keep his word. God responded by turning out all the lights and 24/7 darkness engulfed Egypt.

At this point Pharaoh attempted to negotiate with Moses. The Hebrews could depart but Pharaoh demanded they leave behind their flocks and herds. Pharaoh had previously attempted to persuade Moses to leave their women, children, and livestock behind (Exodus 10:9, 10). On both occasions Moses responded to Pharaoh's proposed compromise in the same manner: "We are not leaving anything or anyone behind."

I think Satan is still pitching the same deal to twenty-first century followers of Christ. "You can go on with God if you must, but leave your family and friends behind with me." I pray that your response is the same one Moses used with Pharaoh: "No deal devil! We will go with our young and our old; all our sons and our daughters; our family and our friends--we are not willing to leave anyone behind for you."

Exodus Chapter 11   One last time Moses returned to Pharaoh to deliver God's ultimatum. If Pharaoh refused to let God's people go, every firstborn son and animal in Egypt would die; including Pharaoh's son. Pharaoh responded by hardening his heart, and again refusing to comply with God's command.

Exodus Chapter 12   God always says what He means and means what He says. He intends for mankind to take whatever He requires of us seriously. God made provision for all Egyptians or Hebrews who followed His instructions to be passed over by His death angel. A perfect one-year-old male lamb or sheep was to be sacrificed, roasted over a fire, and entirely eaten by each family unit. Some of the blood from the sacrificial animal was to be put on the sides and tops of each home's doorframes. Every family member was required to remain inside the homes that had been properly protected, throughout the entire night.

Please notice that God's instructions were specific and needed to be carefully and completely carried out. Close only counts with horseshoes and hand grenades; not compliance with God's commands. Faith always requires doing exactly what God instructs us to do, when and where He tells us to do it.

"At midnight the LORD struck down all the firstborn in the land of Egypt, from the firstborn of Pharaoh who sat on his throne to the firstborn of the captive who was in the dungeon, and all the firstborn of the livestock. And Pharaoh rose up in the night, he and all his servants and all the Egyptians. And there was a great cry in Egypt, for there was not a house where someone was not dead." **Exodus 12:29, 30**

Finally, God's purposeful plagues broke Pharaoh's hold on His people.

"Then he summoned Moses and Aaron by night and said, 'Up, go out from among my people, both you and the people of Israel; and go, serve the LORD, as you have said. Take your flocks and your herds, as you have said, and be gone, and bless me also.' The Egyptians were urgent with the people to send them out of the land in haste. For they said, 'We shall all be dead.'" **Exodus 12:31-33**

The Promise Land Principle
CHAPTER 5

Faith's Learning Laboratory

Exodus chapter 12 closes with Moses in the lead U-Haul singing, "On the road again, like a band of gypsies we go down the highway."

No one can say with certainty how many Israelites left Egypt with Moses. We do know, however, that there were over six hundred thousand Hebrew men (Exodus 12:37; Numbers 1: 46; Numbers 26: 51). It seems certain that more than a million Hebrews participated in the Exodus adventure.

I believe everything that occurred during the estimated two year journey of the Hebrews from captivity in Egypt to arriving at God's open door of opportunity in Canaan was planned or permitted by God to prepare the faith they required to take possession of their promise land. Their journey through the wilderness provided several faith learning laboratory lessons.

Faith Learning Laboratory Lesson 1   God is Our Protector

We remember that the Israelites were being led by God's Shekinah glory cloud during the day and His holy fire by night. God's people ended up in their stressful Red Sea situation because they followed God's leading and directions. Their perilous predicament was clearly engineered by God to achieve His particular purpose.

"Then the LORD said to Moses, 'Tell the people of Israel to turn back and encamp in front of Pi-hahiroth, between Migdol and the sea, in front of Baal-zephon; you shall encamp facing it, by the sea. For Pharaoh will say of the people of Israel, 'They are wandering in the land; the wilderness has shut them in.' And I will harden Pharaoh's heart, and he will pursue them, and I will get glory over Pharaoh and all his host, and the Egyptians shall know that I am the LORD.' And they did so." **Exodus 14:1-4**

Why in the world would God put His own people in harm's way? Apparently He felt this was the most effective method of teaching them to trust Him. How has God gone about developing trust and faith in your life?

The king of Egypt took the bait and mobilized his army. Off they went in hot pursuit of God's people. The Egyptians found them apparently trapped, right where God had put them; time for some payback.

"When Pharaoh drew near, the people of Israel lifted up their eyes, and behold, the Egyptians were marching after them, and they feared greatly. And the people of Israel cried out to the LORD. They said to Moses, 'Is it because there are no graves in Egypt that you have taken us away to die in the wilderness? What have you done to us in bringing us out of Egypt? Is not this what we said to you in Egypt: 'Leave us alone that we may serve the Egyptians'? For it would have been better for us to serve the Egyptians than to die in the wilderness.'" **Exodus 14:10-12**

I'm sad to say that the Hebrews flunked God's one question pop quiz: "What do you do when you find yourself trapped between a rock and a hard spot?" Their answer: panic, blame, and complain!

Those of us who have read the end of this story, or have seen the movie "The Ten Commandments," or the animated version "The Prince of Egypt", want to shout out to the Hebrews, "Relax! God's got your back!" But put yourself in their place; their situation seemed hopeless. Are there any similar situations that you have personally experienced; times when, if God had not come through, you would have been a goner?

Moses responded to this situation in the manner God desires of all leaders whom He has enlisted to function by faith.

"Moses said to the people, 'Fear not, stand firm, and see the salvation of the LORD, which He will work for you today. For the Egyptians whom you see today, you shall never see again. The LORD will fight for you, and you have only to be silent.'" **Exodus 14:13, 14**

Using some sanctified imagination, I visualize Moses saying to God at this point, "'I AM', we really need to talk about this situation." God responds by saying something like, "What seems to be the problem?" Moses replies, "Well it's like this; on my left is this sea that is too deep to wade through, and too wide to swim across. On my right is this angry army with our blood in their eyes." God's answer: "Moses, whose problem is this; Mine or yours?" Moses isn't completely satisfied with God's answer. "I suppose it's Your problem, however, I would be extremely interested in knowing what You intend to do about Your problem?"

"The LORD said to Moses, 'Why do you cry to Me? Tell the people of Israel to go forward. Lift up your staff, and stretch out your hand over the sea and divide it, that the people of Israel may go through the sea on dry ground. And I will harden the hearts of the Egyptians so that they shall go in after them, and I will get glory over Pharaoh and all his host, his chariots, and his horsemen. And the Egyptians shall know that I am the LORD, when I have gotten glory over Pharaoh, his chariots, and his horsemen.'" **Exodus 14:15-18**

God was waiting for Moses and the Hebrews to start functioning by faith; to begin believing, trusting and depending upon Him. "Go forward by faith! Raise your rod, man of God!"

When Moses and the people of God did what God instructed them to do, God came through as He promised them He always would. The sea opened, God's path of protection appeared, the Hebrews were delivered and delighted, while all the pursuing Egyptians were drowned and destroyed.

"The people of Israel walked on dry ground through the sea, the waters being a wall to them on their right hand and on their left. Thus the LORD saved Israel that day from the hand of the Egyptians, and Israel saw the Egyptians dead on the seashore. Israel saw the great power that the LORD used against the Egyptians, so the people feared the LORD, and they believed in the LORD and in His servant Moses." **Exodus 14:29-31**

Faith Learning Laboratory Lesson 2   God is Our Provider

Faith is always about doing what God tells you to do, when He tells you to do it, where He tells you to do it, and how He tells you to do it.

As the Israelites begin the next leg of their journey they soon encounter two more problems: No water, and no food. These are obviously things that they required. So how did they go about getting what they needed?

The Israelites find themselves traveling through the Desert of Shur where there are no fast food diners, or grocery stores. When they arrive at a place called Marah, they do find a pond, but its water is too bitter to drink. Sadly, God's guys and gals are not yet ready to deal with getting their needs met by faith.

"The people grumbled against Moses, saying, 'What shall we drink?'" **Exodus 15:24**

Constantly complaining whenever we don't get what we want or think we need is a hard habit for some people to break. God has given us instructions concerning how to get what He feels we need, by faith.

"Ask, and it will be given to you; seek, and you will find; knock, and it will be opened to you." **Matthew 7:7**

"You do not have, because you do not ask." **James 4:2**

When Moses asked God to provide water for His people, God accommodated his request. "He cried to the LORD, and the LORD showed him a log, and he threw it into the water, and the water became sweet." **Exodus 15:25**

The Hebrews next moved to Elim, and then traveled into the Desert of Sin. The location of the Hebrews changed daily while their constant complaining continued without change.

"They set out from Elim, and all the congregation of the people of Israel came to the wilderness of Sin, which is between Elim and Sinai, on the fifteenth day of the second month after they had departed from the land of Egypt. And the whole congregation of the people of Israel grumbled against Moses and Aaron in the wilderness, and the people of Israel said to them, 'Would that we had died by the hand of the LORD in the land of Egypt, when we sat by the meat pots and ate bread to the full, for you have brought us out into this wilderness to kill this whole assembly with hunger.'" **Exodus 16:1-3**

This time, God quickly steps in and tells Moses, "I hear all the moaning, groaning, and grumbling. I'll handle it." God proceeds to miraculously provide daily flat bread falling from the sky called manna. God's manna came with instructions that weren't always followed. Whenever the Hebrews failed to comply with God's commands, the manna became infested with worms. Additionally, God caused quail to drop in at their camp for dinner, and fresh water to flow from rocks. The Israelites were able to eat and drink their fill, as long as they followed God's instructions by faith.

Faith Learning Laboratory Lesson 3 God's People Prevail by Means of His Power and Plan

The Israelites next faith training exercise involved war with the Amalekites. It is noted that the Amalekites picked the fight but God finished it. Moses was given a battle plan that military strategists might consider slightly unorthodox. Success, as usual, was all about following God's instructions by faith.

"Moses said to Joshua, 'Choose for us men, and go out and fight with Amalek. Tomorrow I will stand on the top of the hill with the staff of God in my hand.' So Joshua did as Moses told him, and fought with Amalek, while Moses, Aaron, and Hur went up to the top of the hill. Whenever Moses held up his hand, Israel prevailed, and whenever he lowered his hand, Amalek prevailed. But Moses' hands grew weary, so they took a stone and put it under him, and he sat on it, while Aaron and Hur held up his hands, one on one side, and the other on the other side. So his hands were steady until the going down of the sun. And Joshua overwhelmed Amalek and his people with the sword." **Exodus 17:9-13**

Apparently it was important to God that you and I learn how His guys won this fight by faith because He instructed Moses to include it in the book he would later write under the inspiration of the Holy Spirit (**Exodus 17:14**).

Faith Learning Laboratory Lesson 4   Leaders Must Keep Listening and Learning

Exodus 18 finds Moses making a common leadership mistake; he seems to think that he is indispensable. Apparently he slept through his seminary class on delegating responsibility. Long lines of Hebrews waited all day to talk with him.

"Moses sat to judge the people, and the people stood around Moses from morning till evening. When Moses' father-in-law saw all that he was doing for the people, he said, 'What is this that you are doing for the people? Why do you sit alone, and all the people stand around you from morning till evening?' And Moses said to his father-in-law, 'Because the people come to me to inquire of God; when they have a dispute, they come to me and I decide between one person and another, and I make them know the statutes of God and his laws.'" **Exodus 18:13-16**

His father-in-law Jethro provided him with some awesome leadership counseling. "Son, you are going to wear yourself and all these people out if you continue what you are doing. God never intended for you to carry out the assignment He gave you all by yourself. You need enlist and equip some other leaders and delegate most of these responsibilities to them. Teamwork makes the dream work!"

"'Now obey my voice; I will give you advice, and God be with you! You shall represent the people before God and bring their cases to God, and you shall warn them about the statutes and the laws, and make them know the way in which they must walk and what they must do. Moreover, look for able men from all the people, men who fear God, who are trustworthy and hate a bribe, and place such men over the people as chiefs of thousands, of hundreds, of fifties, and of tens. And let them judge the people at all times. Every great matter they shall bring to you, but any small matter they shall decide themselves. So it will be easier for you, and they will bear the burden with you. If you do this, God will direct you, you will be able to endure, and all this people also will go to their place in peace.' So Moses listened to the voice of his father-in-law and did all that he had said." **Exodus 18:19-24**

As I have previously stated, faith is about following God's instructions. In this case, God's instructions were provided to Moses through his father-in-law Jethro. Moses was the leader, but he was wise enough, and teachable enough, to listen, learn, and change his approach to ministry.

The New Testament provides us with a similar scenario. A problem developed within the early church related to the care of Gentile widows who felt they were being slighted. The Apostles scheduled a special called business meeting.

"The twelve summoned the full number of the disciples and said, 'It is not right that we should give up preaching the word of God to serve tables. Therefore, brothers, pick out from among you seven men of good repute, full of the Spirit and of wisdom, whom we will appoint to this duty. But we will devote ourselves to prayer and to the ministry of the word.'" **Acts 6:2-4**

The primary responsibility of leadership is to enlist, equip, empower, encourage, evaluate, and elevate other followers of Christ; not attempt to be all things to all people (**Ephesians 4:11, 12**).

As a result of handing the situation with the Gentile widows wisely we read: "The word of God continued to increase, and the number of the disciples multiplied greatly in Jerusalem, and a great many of the priests became obedient to the faith." **Acts 6:7**

Faith Learning Laboratory Lesson 5   Don't Do the Crime If You Can't Do the Time

Exodus chapter 19 through 31 documents an extended meeting that took place between God and Moses on Mount Sinai. During this time Moses was given numerous instructions by God concerning how His people were to conduct themselves. At the end of the meeting, God provided Moses with two stone tablets containing His Ten Commandments.

Moses was gone a long time so the Hebrews grew concerned that he wasn't coming back. As a result they proposed an alternative leadership plan to Associate Pastor Aaron.

"Make us gods who shall go before us. As for this Moses, the man who brought us up out of the land of Egypt, we do not know what has become of him." **Exodus 32:1**

As shocking as the request of the Israelites was, even more surprising, at least to me, is the fact that Aaron agreed to accommodate their request. God's people brought their personal gold jewelry to Aaron and he transformed what they brought him into a golden calf. He then proceeded to construct an altar to showcase the carnal cow and scheduled a special feast to supposedly honor the Lord; right!

"They rose up early the next day and offered burnt offerings and brought peace offerings. And the people sat down to eat and drink and rose up to play." **Exodus 32:6**

Their worship service became a drunken orgy. God was extremely upset about the situation and gave Moses a heads up as he headed back to camp carrying the Ten Commandments.

"The LORD said to Moses, 'I have seen this people, and behold, it is a stiff-necked people. Now therefore let Me alone, that My wrath may burn hot against them and I may consume them, in order that I may make a great nation of you.'" **Exodus 32:9, 10**

God told Moses that He was going to destroy all of the Hebrews, but Moses talked Him out of doing that. When Moses arrived back at camp he headed straight for Aaron and confronted him. Aaron's response is incredible; "Don't be mad at me. This sad situation isn't my fault."

"Let not the anger of my lord burn hot. You know the people, that they are set on evil.…..So I said to them, 'Let any who have gold take it off.' So they gave it to me, and I threw it into the fire, and out came this calf." **Exodus 32:22, 24**

The Israelites suffered some immediate consequences for failing to follow God's instructions. About three thousand of those who sinned that day were put to death by the Levites. That wasn't the end of the consequences however.

"The LORD said to Moses, 'Whoever has sinned against me, I will blot out of my book. But now go, lead the people to the place about which I have spoken to you; behold, my angel shall go before you. Nevertheless, in the day when I visit, I will visit their sin upon them.' Then the LORD sent a plague on the people, because they made the calf, the one that Aaron made." **Exodus 32:33-35**

There is always a stiff penalty to pay when God's people fail to follow God's instructions by faith. Don't do the crime, if you can't do the time.

Deal or No Deal?

Finally, after two years of traveling from Egypt to Canaan, and participating in numerous faith learning laboratory training events, God determined that the time had come to open the promise land door of opportunity for the Israelites.

"The LORD said to Moses, 'Depart; go up from here, you and the people whom you have brought up out of the land of Egypt, to the land of which I swore to Abraham, Isaac, and Jacob, saying, "To your offspring I will give it." I will send an angel before you, and I will drive out the Canaanites, the Amorites, the Hittites, the Perizzites, the Hivites, and the Jebusites.'" **Exodus 33:1, 2**

Numbers 13 tells us what occurred after the Israelites arrived at their destination.

"The LORD spoke to Moses, saying, 'Send men to spy out the land of Canaan, which I am giving to the people of Israel. From each tribe of their fathers you shall send a man, every one a chief among them.'" **Numbers 13:1, 2**

The objective of the task force was to obtain strategic information required to develop their game plan for taking possession of their promise land.

Moses gave them instructions concerning their mission in much the same manner as Jesus first commissioned His church (**Matthew 28:18-20**). God never intended for them to use the information they gathered as the basis for deciding whether or not success was feasible; whether or not to follow His instructions.

"Moses sent them to spy out the land of Canaan and said to them, 'Go up into the Negeb and go up into the hill country, and see what the land is, and whether the people who dwell in it are strong or weak, whether they are few or many, and whether the land that they dwell in is good or bad, and whether the cities that they dwell in are camps or strongholds, and whether the land is rich or poor, and whether there are trees in it or not. Be of good courage and bring some of the fruit of the land.' Now the time was the season of the first ripe grapes." **Numbers 13:17-20**

The reconnaissance team spent the next forty days exploring their promise land. They even returned with some grapes, pomegranates, and figs that verified how fantastically fruitful Canaan was. All twelve members of the task force agreed on what they had seen. There was no conflict regarding what they had observed.

The twelve member scouting party was divided, however, concerning their interpretation of the information they brought back with them. Ten of the team members were the first to submit their majority report and recommendations to Moses and the Israelites.

"And they told him, 'We came to the land to which you sent us. It flows with milk and honey, and this is its fruit. However, the people who dwell in the land are strong, and the cities are fortified and very large. And besides, we saw the descendants of Anak there. The Amalekites dwell in the land of the Negeb. The Hittites, the Jebusites, and the Amorites dwell in the hill country. And the Canaanites dwell by the sea, and along the Jordan.'" **Numbers 13:27-29**

No problem thus far. They were merely reporting what they had been sent to observe. Apparently, however, their report caused quite a commotion among the Israelites. At this point, Caleb provided them with the two member minority recommendations.

"But Caleb quieted the people before Moses and said, 'Let us go up at once and occupy it, for we are well able to overcome it.'" **Numbers 13:30**

The people's panic quickly escalated when the majority group made their recommendation.

"Then the men who had gone up with him said, 'We are not able to go up against the people, for they are stronger than we are.' So they brought to the people of Israel a bad report of the land that they had spied out, saying, 'The land, through which we have gone to spy it out, is a land that devours its inhabitants, and all the people that we saw in it are of great height. And there we saw the Nephilim (the sons of Anak, who come from the Nephilim), and we seemed to ourselves like grasshoppers, and so we seemed to them.'" **Numbers 13:31-33**

After all the miracles God pulled off to deliver them from Egyptian captivity, and all the faith lessons they experienced during their Exodus journey, they still flunk God's end of course summative assessment. The answer they wrote on their test paper indicated that they believed it would be better to give into fear rather than go forward by faith. "The obstacles and the opposition are too formidable and fearsome for us to overcome. There is no way we can possibly pull this off!"

"Then all the congregation raised a loud cry, and the people wept that night. And all the people of Israel grumbled against Moses and Aaron. The whole congregation said to them, 'Would that we had died in the land of Egypt! Or would that we had died in this wilderness! Why is the LORD bringing us into this land, to fall by the sword? Our wives and our little ones will become a prey. Would it not be better for us to go back to Egypt?' And they said to one another, 'Let us choose a leader and go back to Egypt.'" **Numbers 14:1-4**

Even if I hadn't yet read the end of this sad scenario, I would feel quite certain that this course of action was not going to turn out well for the

Israelites; choosing fear over faith is a disastrous decision for old covenant Israelites or new covenant followers of Christ.

Four key leaders attempted to reason with the crying, complaining, cowardly crowd.

"Then Moses and Aaron fell on their faces before all the assembly of the congregation of the people of Israel. And Joshua the son of Nun and Caleb the son of Jephunneh, who were among those who had spied out the land, tore their clothes and said to all the congregation of the people of Israel, 'The land, which we passed through to spy it out, is an exceedingly good land. If the LORD delights in us, He will bring us into this land and give it to us, a land that flows with milk and honey. Only do not rebel against the LORD. And do not fear the people of the land, for they are bread for us. Their protection is removed from them, and the LORD is with us; do not fear them.'" **Numbers 14:5-9**

The Hebrews compared their own abilities with the challenge before them and concluded, "No way we can win!" The faithful foursome compared the obstacles and opposition that existed in their promise land with God's abilities and concluded, "No way we can lose!" Faith realizes that many things are impossible for us, but with God, all things are possible (**Matthew 19:26**).

God had promised to drive out the people currently living in Canaan and give the land to the Hebrews. They were still required to do the work and warfare in partnership with God that was necessary to take possession of their promise land, however "I Am" guaranteed their success. "Commit your work to the LORD, and your plans will be established." Proverbs 16:3

This is how faith always functions. The Israelites, however, decided to decline God's deal, and would have put the faithful four to death had God not intervened.

"Then all the congregation said to stone them with stones. But the glory of the LORD appeared at the tent of meeting to all the people of Israel. And the LORD said to Moses, 'How long will this people despise Me? And

how long will they not believe in Me, in spite of all the signs that I have done among them? I will strike them with the pestilence and disinherit them, and I will make of you a nation greater and mightier than they.'"
Numbers 14:10-12

Fortunately, Moses was able to talk God out of destroying the Hebrews due to their unwillingness to believe and trust Him. Making the wrong choice at the crossroads of fear and faith, however, put them on the road to ruin, rather than the path to the promise land.

"Then the LORD said (to Moses), 'I have pardoned, according to your word. But truly, as I live, and as all the earth shall be filled with the glory of the LORD, none of the men who have seen My glory and My signs that I did in Egypt and in the wilderness, and yet have put Me to the test these ten times and have not obeyed My voice, shall see the land that I swore to give to their fathers. And none of those who despised Me shall see it.'"
Numbers 14:20-23

And that wasn't all God had to say to these faithless followers. He was seriously upset with their lack of trust and obedience.

"And the LORD spoke to Moses and to Aaron, saying, 'How long shall this wicked congregation grumble against Me? I have heard the grumblings of the people of Israel, which they grumble against Me.' Say to them, 'As I live, declares the LORD, what you have said in My hearing I will do to you: your dead bodies shall fall in this wilderness, and of all your number, listed in the census from twenty years old and upward, who have grumbled against Me, not one shall come into the land where I swore that I would make you dwell, except Caleb the son of Jephunneh and Joshua the son of Nun. But your little ones, who you said would become a prey, I will bring in, and they shall know the land that you have rejected. But as for you, your dead bodies shall fall in this wilderness. And your children shall be shepherds in the wilderness forty years and shall suffer for your faithlessness, until the last of your dead bodies lies in the wilderness. According to the number of the days in which you spied out the land, forty days, a year for each day, you shall bear your iniquity forty years, and you shall know my displeasure.' 'I, the LORD, have spoken. Surely this will I do to all this wicked congregation who are gathered together against Me: in this wilderness they shall come to a full end, and there they shall die.' And the men whom Moses sent to spy out the land, who returned and made all the congregation grumble against him by bringing up a bad report about the land— the men who brought up a bad report of the land—died by plague before the LORD. Of those men who went to spy out the land, only Joshua the son of Nun and Caleb the son of Jephunneh remained alive." **Numbers 14:26-38**

For the next forty years every Hebrew adult who left Egypt with Moses wandered in the wilderness east of their promise land and eventually died there. God's door of opportunity for all of them, with the exception of Joshua and Caleb, remained forever closed. The writer of the New Testament book of Hebrews provides some additional insight taken from Israel's wilderness wandering experience; including the description of any refusal to follow where God leads Christ's followers by faith as unbelief, disobedience, and rebellion.

"Today, if you hear His (God's) voice, do not harden your hearts as in the rebellion. For who were those who heard and yet rebelled? Was it not all those who left Egypt led by Moses? And with whom was He provoked for forty years? Was it not with those who sinned, whose bodies fell in the wilderness? And to whom did He swear that they would not enter His rest, but to those who were disobedient? So we see that they were unable to enter (their promise land) because of unbelief." **Hebrews 3:15-19**

Wandering in the Wilderness

Educators use two forms of assessment: formative and summative.

The goal of formative assessment is to monitor student learning to provide ongoing feedback that can be used by instructors to improve their teaching and by students to improve their learning.

More specifically, formative assessments:

- help students identify their strengths and weaknesses and target areas that need more work.
- help teachers and administrators recognize areas of learning deficiency so that those topics can be retaught and relearned.

The goal of summative assessment is to evaluate student learning at the end of an instructional unit by comparing it against some standard or benchmark.

God uses various tests and permits temptation as formative and summative assessment tools to evaluate our learning. We reveal what we have actually learned by the choices we make during the times of testing and temptation. It is our choices that reveal whether God can trust us or not; whether we are willing to believe the promises and apply the principles He has given us. Faith that hasn't been tested, can't be trusted.

If our choice is correct, we receive God's blessing; God's promise land. If our mid-course choices are incorrect, we're required to relearn God's lesson, and take a makeup test. If however, our end-of-course choice is incorrect, we may well end up having to repeat the entire course.

After flunking their end-of-course summative assessment, the Israelites were required to wander in the wilderness east of their promise land for the next forty years.

I've always felt a great subtitle for the Bible would be: "How to Turn God's Promises and Principles into Provisions." Notice what the Bible says about itself,

"All Scripture is breathed out by God and profitable for teaching, for reproof, for correction, and for training in righteousness, that the man of God may be complete, equipped for every good work." **2 Timothy 3:16, 17**

The Israelites had obviously not learned the faith lessons that God had tried to teach them during their Exodus journey. As a result they refused to trust in His promises, and put His principles into practice; as required to possess their promise land. Thus, they choose trudging through the wilderness over thriving in their promise land. The only reason for their failure was their refusal to trust and obey God. They chose not to follow God's instructions and comply with His commands. The decided to do what they believed to be best. They fled in fear rather than followed by faith. The consequences for their wrong choice were catastrophic. Twenty-first century Christians, local churches and Christian organizations need to learn the lessons taught by their travels, tests, trials, temptations, tragedies, and eventual triumphs.

The events that took place during the forty years that the Israelites wandered aimlessly in the desert are described in Numbers 15 thru 36. During this period of time everyone who was twenty years of age or older when the Hebrews turned down their promise land perished; with the exception of Joshua and Caleb.

While wandering in the wilderness, Moses was bombarded by the continual murmurings, grumblings, and complaints of the Israelites. At one point, Moses' patience reached its breaking point and he sinned against the Lord, by reacting in anger to the annoying attitudes of God's people. When the Israelites again began to gripe and grumble saying they had no water, the Lord instructed Moses to speak to a rock and water would be provided. Instead, Moses lifted his hand and struck the rock twice with his rod. Because he disobeyed and disrespected the Lord through this angry act, Moses was not permitted to enter Canaan (Numbers 20:1-13). The privilege of leading the Israelites into their promise land would belong to his successor, Joshua.

Some of the other more notable events that occurred during the forty years of wilderness wandering are as follows:

- The rebellion of Korah and others against the leadership of Moses. God responded by opening the earth and swallowing up everyone who followed Korah. **Numbers 16:1-35**
- Aaron's rod budded and bore almonds. In this way God made known His selection of Aaron and the tribe of Levi as His special servants who were authorized to speak for Him. **Numbers 17:1-10**
- The death of Moses sister Miriam and brother Aaron. **Numbers 20:1; 23-29; 33:28, 29**
- Fiery serpents and a brass serpent on a pole. This was a lesson intended to teach the Israelites that faith is always a better response than complaining about our circumstances. **Numbers 21:4-9**
- Balaam is hired as an independent contractor by the Moabites to figure out a way to have Israel cursed rather than blessed by God. His plan demonstrates that sex is an extremely effective method of seducing God's people into sin. **Numbers 22:1 thru 24:5**
- A plague sent by God destroys twenty-four thousand idolatrous Israelites. **Numbers 25:1-9**
- Moses dies at age 120 (**Deuteronomy 34:9**). I find it significant that eighty years of his life were spent in two different wilderness areas, and he never entered God's promise land. Impulsiveness and anger can take you out of God's game, put you on the bench, and cause you to miss out on God's blessing. Let those who have ears to hear, hear.

Decision Driven Destinations

God wants Christ's followers to trust in His promises and apply the principles that He inspired to be written in the Bible. The decision to trust and obey God guarantees that we will eventually end up in our promise land. Our decisions determine our direction, our direction will eventually determine our destination, and our destination will ultimately determine our destiny. I often ask those who appear to be wandering in some wilderness, "When you get to where you're going, where will you be?"

"If you don't know where you are going, any road will get you there." Lewis Carroll

If God's people individually or corporately choose fear over faith, as the Israelites did during the first opportunity they were given to enter their promise land, and disregard God's invitation or disobey God's instructions, we will soon find ourselves on the way to some wilderness.

The choice is ours to make. The consequence, delight or disaster, is always a direct result of our decisions at the critical crossroads of our Jesus journey.

The good news that comes from the Exodus story is that after forty years of wilderness wandering, God gave the Israelites a second opportunity to claim their promise land. God led His people back to the Jordan River east of Canaan and proceeded to commission Joshua; the man He selected to replace Moses.

"After the death of Moses the servant of the LORD, the LORD said to Joshua the son of Nun, Moses' assistant, 'Moses My servant is dead. Now therefore arise, go over this Jordan, you and all this people, into the land that I am giving to them, to the people of Israel. Every place that the sole of your foot will tread upon I have given to you, just as I promised to Moses. From the wilderness and this Lebanon as far as the great river, the river Euphrates, all the land of the Hittites to the Great Sea toward the going down of the sun shall be your territory. No man shall be able to stand before you all the days of your life. Just as I was with Moses, so I will be with you. I will not leave you or forsake you. Be strong and courageous, for you shall cause this people to inherit the land that I swore to their fathers to give them. Only be strong and very courageous, being careful to do according to all the law that Moses my servant commanded you. Do not turn from it to the right hand or to the left, that you may have good success wherever you go. This Book of the Law shall not depart from your mouth, but you shall meditate on it day and night, so that you may be careful to do according to all that is written in it. For then you will make your way prosperous, and then you will have good success. Have I not commanded you? Be strong and courageous. Do not be frightened, and do not be dismayed, for the LORD your God is with you wherever you go.'" **Joshua 1:1-9**

I want to make sure you understand what God required of the Israelites; in particular their leaders. I also want to stress for you what God promised related to the process of taking possession of their promise land.

What God required of the Israelites in order to possess their promise land.

- The Hebrews were required to proactively perform all of the necessary work and warfare assigned to them by God.

- God told them to be strong in faith and courageous in battle. They were not to make any decisions based upon fear, worry, doubt, or discouragement.
- The Israelites were commanded to learn, live, and labor according to God's guidelines. Their Commander-in-Chief stressed that His people were required to obey all of His "whats, whens, wheres, and hows."

The provision and protection God promised to provide for the Israelites as they went about the task of possessing their promise land.

- God guaranteed that He would give His people all of their promise land that they set their feet upon by faith.
- No opposition or obstacles existing within the boundaries of their promise land would be able to prevent them from taking possession of it.
- God promised to be with them wherever they went while they were in the process of possessing their property; He would never leave or forsake His people.
- The outcome of their faith endeavor was guaranteed by God to be totally successful if they complied with His commands; all of them.

I believe this is exactly the same deal God is offering twenty-first century followers of Christ, local churches, and Christian organizations as we go about the process of taking possession of the various mission fields God has assigned us. Stop and take another look at our part and God's part in this process before you proceed.

At the beginning of the twenty-first century I served as church planter for a congregation started by eleven adults. We began with few resources and no facility. As we prayed and planned for the start of our ministry God brought us to the promise He had first made to Joshua. "Every place that the sole of your foot will tread upon I have given to you, just as I promised to Moses." **Joshua 1:3**

We all believed that God intended for us to claim this promise and proactively put it into practice by faith related to our promise land; our primary area of mission responsibility.

We began by defining the boundaries of our promise land. We carefully, and prayerfully marked it out on a map. We next divided the first area up it up into five separate sections of 250 homes which teams comprised of two church members (married couples where possible) were assigned responsibility for. We each viewed ourselves as the primary "Foot of Faith" missionaries for our assigned territories.

We regularly prayed for our assigned territories and four to six times each year walked every street while praying for the homes, leaving professionally prepared promotional materials, and when possible meeting the residents. As our church membership grew, our number of 250 home promise land territories increased and were assigned to additional "Foot of Faith" missionaries.

As He had done for Joshua, God worked in partnership with us and abundantly blessed our "Foot of Faith" outreach. During the years I served as lead pastor our congregation grew increasingly excited about the impact of their missionary work and the success we regularly experienced and celebrated.

After his meeting with God, Joshua didn't schedule a special called business meeting in order to vote on whether or not to go forward by faith. He presented the victorious vision he had been given to God's people.

"Joshua commanded the officers of the people, 'Pass through the midst of the camp and command the people to prepare your provisions, for within three days you are to pass over this Jordan to go in to take possession of the land that the LORD your God is giving you to possess.'" **Joshua 1:10, 11**

This time, the Israelites responded in faith rather than fear.

"They (the Israelites) answered Joshua, 'All that you have commanded us we will do, and wherever you send us we will go. Just as we obeyed Moses in all things, so we will obey you. Only may the LORD your God be with you, as He was with Moses! Whoever rebels against your commandment and disobeys your words, whatever you command him, shall be put to death. Only be strong and courageous.'" **Joshua 1:16-18**

What pastor wouldn't jump for joy by receiving that vote of confidence from their congregation? The first church I was given the privilege to serve as lead Pastor was a small rural congregation that I drove to on the weekends while attending seminary. The chairman of our deacons, whose name was Ben Ogilvie, said to me, "Pastor, you lead us where God wants us to go, and we will follow." Imagine what an encouragement that was to me as I began my ministry at that church.

Joshua next proceeds to send a two member scouting party to check out the city of Jericho; the place where their first promise land battle took place. Joshua knew about Jericho from his previous forty day exploration of the promise land. The two scouts return with an optimistic report: "Truly the LORD has given all the land into our hands. And also, all the inhabitants of the land melt away because of us." **Joshua 2:24**

Before taking on Jericho, however, Joshua and the Israelites encountered another major obstacle blocking their path of progress. The Jordan River had to be crossed during the time of year it was at flood stage. This normally occurs annually in late April or early May.

Joshua tells God's guys and gals to get ready to cross the river; the priests, carrying the Ark of the Covenant, are required to take the first steps into the water. What amazes me is that no one seemed to have any doubts about getting to the other side of the raging river. Right on schedule God came through as He had promised to do.

"As soon as those bearing the ark had come as far as the Jordan, and the feet of the priests bearing the ark were dipped in the brink of the water (now the Jordan overflows all its banks throughout the time of harvest), the waters coming down from above stood and rose up in a heap very far away, at Adam, the city that is beside Zarethan, and those flowing down toward the Sea of the Arabah, the Salt Sea, were completely cut off. And the people passed over opposite Jericho. Now the priests bearing the ark of the covenant of the LORD stood firmly on dry ground in the midst of the Jordan, and all Israel was passing over on dry ground until all the nation finished passing over the Jordan." **Joshua 3:15-17**

You and I have an open invitation to enter and possess that land God wants to give us. In order for that to happen we must learn to trust and obey God. It is essential that dependency upon His promises and principles become more than Bible Study group discussion and spiritual lip service. If we want to walk on water with Jesus, we must be willing to leave the comfort zones that we have carefully crafted; before we can walk on water we have to be willing to get out of the boat. We must be willing, as the Israelites were, to step into the water, and wade out a little bit deeper.

Awaiting Joshua and the Israelites on the western side of the Jordan River was another major challenge; the walled city of Jericho.

"Now Jericho was shut up inside and outside because of the people of Israel. None went out, and none came in." **Joshua 6:1**

The residents of the city responded to the Israelite threat by closing the city gates and guarding them. The massive walls surrounding the city seemed impenetrable.

The total area occupied by the city of Jericho is believed to have been about six acres. It is estimated that the population at that time would have been approximately 2500 people.

God provided Joshua with a strategic battle plan that guaranteed a victorious outcome. Here again we notice how important it was for God's specific instructions to be carefully followed by faith. Please understand that God always says exactly what He means and means exactly what He says. If Joshua or the Israelites had not completely complied with God's instructions, they would have failed; as they eventually did at Ai due to the sin of Achan (Joshua 7). Sins of commission and omission are always the result of someone's failure to follow God's instructions.

"The LORD said to Joshua, 'See, I have given Jericho into your hand, with its king and mighty men of valor. You shall march around the city, all the men of war going around the city once. Thus shall you do for six days. Seven priests shall bear seven trumpets of rams' horns before the ark. On the seventh day you shall march around the city seven times, and the priests shall blow the trumpets. And when they make a long blast with the ram's horn, when you hear the sound of the trumpet, then all the people shall shout with a great shout, and the wall of the city will fall down flat, and the people shall go up, everyone straight before him.'" **Joshua 6:2-5**

Amazingly the Israelites finally decided to do what God wanted, the way God instructed them to; by faith. For seven days they marched around Jericho doing exactly what God required them to do. As a result of their complete, and cooperative compliance, God gave them the city.

"So the people shouted, and the trumpets were blown. As soon as the people heard the sound of the trumpet, the people shouted a great shout, and the wall fell down flat, so that the people went up into the city, every man straight before him, and they captured the city. Then they devoted all in the city to destruction, both men and women, young and old, oxen, sheep, and donkeys, with the edge of the sword." **Joshua 6:20, 21**

God, however, had also given them instructions concerning how He wanted them to deal with the assets taken from the city.

"Keep yourselves from the things devoted to destruction, lest when you have devoted them you take any of the devoted things and make the camp of Israel a thing for destruction and bring trouble upon it. But all silver and gold, and every vessel of bronze and iron, are holy to the LORD; they shall go into the treasury of the LORD." **Joshua 6:18, 19**

Joshua 7 opens with an all too familiar sad scenario, "The Israelites did not obey the Lord." **Joshua 7:1**

A man named Achan from the tribe of Judah, kept some of the Lord's loot for himself and caused God to again become upset at the Israelites. As a result, when Joshua sent three thousand soldiers to make quick work of the seemingly defenseless city of Ai, the Israelites, to their surprise and dismay, were soundly defeated.

I love the conversation Joshua had with God after the Hebrew warriors were defeated. I have had a few of these conversations with God myself during my years of local church leadership.

"Then Joshua tore his clothes and fell to the earth on his face before the ark of the LORD until the evening, he and the elders of Israel. And they put dust on their heads. And Joshua said, 'Alas, O LORD God, why have you brought this people over the Jordan at all, to give us into the hands of the Amorites, to destroy us? Would that we had been content to dwell beyond the Jordan! O Lord, what can I say, when Israel has turned their backs before their enemies! For the Canaanites and all the inhabitants of the land will hear of it and will surround us and cut off our name from the earth. And what will You do for Your great name?'" **Joshua 7:6-9**

Joshua's question to God should not have been, "God what is the deal with you letting this happen to us?" But rather, "God what did I/we do wrong that resulted in this defeat?"

Read carefully what God required Joshua to do in order to restore His blessing.

"The LORD said to Joshua, 'Get up! Why have you fallen on your face? Israel has sinned; they have transgressed my covenant that I commanded them; they have taken some of the devoted things; they have stolen and lied and put them among their own belongings. Therefore the people of Israel cannot stand before their enemies. They turn their backs before their enemies, because they have become devoted for destruction. I will be with you no more, unless you destroy the devoted things from among you. Get up! Consecrate the people and say, Consecrate yourselves for tomorrow; for thus says the LORD, God of Israel, There are devoted things in your midst, O Israel. You cannot stand before your enemies until you take away the devoted things from among you.'" **Joshua 7:10-13**

"Joshua, My people have again disobeyed Me. They have disregarded My instructions and treated Me with defiant disrespect. Until you deal with this problem there won't be any further protection or provision for those I have placed under your leadership."

I encourage every church leader reading this section of the promise land story to at least consider the possibly that dealing with these types of problems which occur within the membership of local churches is far more essential than we may understand or want to believe. I realize many local church leaders have no desire to confront carnality within their congregations; some even dread dealing with church discipline issues. I contend however, that ignoring sin within the household of God will adversely impact God's blessing upon your ministry.

When it was discovered that Achan had taken treasure from Jericho and hid it in his tent, God required that his entire family, and everything he owned be destroyed.

"Then the LORD turned from His burning anger....And the LORD said to Joshua, 'Do not fear and do not be dismayed. Take all the fighting men with you, and arise, go up to Ai. See, I have given into your hand the king of Ai, and his people, his city, and his land.'" **Joshua 7:26-8:1**

I want to look at another amazing thing God did to help His people take possession of their promise land. This event is described in Joshua 10 where we find Joshua and his soldiers engaged in combat with a coalition comprised of five Amorite armies. Joshua is winning the battle but as the day draws to an end he finds that he needs a little more time to obtain victory. So Joshua prays and asks God to have the sun stand still over the city of Gibeon where the battle is taking place, and God accommodates his request.

"The sun stopped in the midst of heaven and did not hurry to set for about a whole day. There has been no day like it before or since, when the LORD heeded the voice of a man, for the LORD fought for Israel." **Joshua 10:13, 14**

Since Joshua was confident that the Israelites were properly plugged into God's purpose and plan, he had no problem asking for God's help; asking for an amazing miracle. Isn't that exactly what Jesus encouraged His followers to do?

"Whatever you ask in My name, this I will do, that the Father may be glorified in the Son. If you ask Me for anything in My name, I will do it." **John 14:13, 14**

I think the type of asking and expecting faith demonstrated by Joshua is at the root of what Jesus meant when he said, "If you had faith like a grain of mustard seed, you could say to this mulberry tree, 'Be uprooted and planted in the sea,' and it would obey you." **Luke 17:6**

By carrying out their assigned work and warfare in partnership with God, the Israelites eventually were able to possess their promise land. Years later, as Joshua was preparing to step down from leadership, he encouraged God's people to always remember the source of their success.

"For the LORD has driven out before you great and strong nations. And as for you, no man has been able to stand before you to this day. One man of you puts to flight a thousand, since it is the LORD your God who fights for you, just as He promised you." **Joshua 23:9, 10**

The promise land principle requires that we learn to believe, trust, and depend upon God in order to fulfill His intended purpose and plans for our life and labor on earth by faith. The entire Exodus story is about God delivering and preparing a people to function as His partners in accomplishing His purpose; people who are willing to follow His instructions and put His will ahead of their own aims, agendas, opinions, and preferences.

I believe God is still operating in the lives of Christ's followers and local churches based upon "The Promise Land Principle". In the three concluding chapters of this book I want to point out to you that God is still delivering people from captivity for the primary purpose of preparing them to partner with Him by faith in possessing our promise lands.

CHAPTER 9

Set Free from Slavery to Sin

The Israelites didn't purposefully relocate to Egypt to be enslaved, nor were they taken there as captives. They were invited to Egypt and at first, because of Joseph, they were treated extremely well. Their first few years of living in Egypt as guests were pleasurable.

No one drinking their first beer does so intending to become an alcoholic. Who puffs on their first marijuana joint hoping to end up dealing with drug addiction? Does anyone ever apply for their first credit card anticipating future residency in some dungeon of debt? For a time, their existence in Egypt was extremely enjoyable for the Israelites. Likewise, alcohol, drugs, and debt are initially pleasurable for many people. Seductive sin may provide satisfaction for a season (**Hebrews 11:25**). Eventually, however, we find ourselves being held captive by debt, illness, depression, or some addiction.

The source of sin is our independent self-centeredness; choosing our will and way over God's. God created us to live in relationship with Him; depending upon Him for many things. Sin causes us to choose what self wants or believes to be best over God's commands, counsel, instructions, wisdom, truth, and purpose for our lives. Our declarations of independence from God always result in captive consequences.

God has placed warnings throughout Scripture concerning the need to totally trust Him rather than our own limited understanding, flawed wisdom, or personal preferences; what we believe to be best. "Trust in the LORD with all your heart, and do not lean on your own understanding. In all your ways acknowledge him, and he will make straight your paths." **Proverbs 3:5, 6**

Jesus came to do for us what we could not possibly do for ourselves; what God sent Moses to do for the Israelites. The mission of Jesus was to initially set us free from the penalty and prison of sin. When He exited earth, He sent the Holy Spirit to progressively set His followers free from the power of sin; to lead us by faith into our various promise lands. Jesus came to provide us with the opportunity to restore our relationship with God and learn to live and labor as we were originally created; in trust and dependence upon God, and obedience to God.

The commission Christ entrusted to His church, in partnership with the Holy Spirit, involves rescuing people from spiritual captivity to sin and Satan, restoring their relationship with their Father and His family, training them to live, love, and labor by faith, leading them to their promise land, and helping them take full possession of it.

I believe Jesus was referencing the promise land principle when He spoke about His redemptive mission.

"The thief comes only to steal and kill and destroy. I came that they may have life and have it abundantly." **John 10:10**

The story line of sin and salvation begins in Genesis and continues throughout all sixty-six books of the Bible. God created the world and gave the human race He created instructions concerning our existence on earth. At one time or another, we have all sinned by disobeying or disregarding God's instructions as Adam and Eve first did (**Genesis 3:23**).

Immediately after creating the earth and the first human named Adam, God said to him, "Adam, let me see your eyeballs. I have some very important instructions that you need to hear and heed."

"The Lord God commanded the man, saying, 'You may surely eat of every tree of the garden, but of the tree of the knowledge of good and evil you shall not eat, for in the day that you eat of it you shall surely die.'" **Genesis 2:16, 17**

Adam was permitted to eat of any tree in the Garden of Eden with one exception. That seems extremely reasonable; right? A vast number of fruit bearing trees were provided to satisfy Adam's hunger. Just don't eat from the tree whose fruit brings about the knowledge of good and evil. God clearly stated what the consequences would be for disregarding and disobeying His instructions; instant death.

The immediate death God spoke to Adam about wasn't physical death, but rather spiritual death. The Bible states that God made mankind in His likeness and image (**Genesis 1:27**). We were originally created as three-dimensional beings possessing a physical body, an eternal soul, and a spirit (**1 Thessalonians 5:23; Hebrews 4:12**). It is man's spirit that enables him to experience a spiritual relationship with God Who has revealed Himself to mankind as Father, Son, and Holy Spirit.

Since the creation of the earth and mankind, the penalty for even one sin (failing to follow God's instructions and/or comply with His commands) has been instant spiritual death and termination of our relationship with God (**Romans 6:23**).

Soon after creating Adam God created Eve to be a companion and helper for him. **Genesis 3** opens with Eve standing at the forbidden tree with her husband, listening to a slick satanic sin sales presentation.

"Now the serpent was more crafty than any other beast of the field that the Lord God had made. He said to the woman, 'Did God actually say, You shall not eat of any tree in the garden?' And the woman said to the serpent, 'We may eat of the fruit of the trees in the garden, but God said, You shall not eat of the fruit of the tree that is in the midst of the garden, neither shall you touch it, lest you die.' But the serpent said to the woman, 'You will not surely die. For God knows that when you eat of it your eyes will be opened and you will be like God, knowing good and evil.'" **Genesis 3:1-5**

So what would Eve do? She knew what God had told them not to do. She even embellished God's instructions claiming He had told them to not even touch the fruit. Satan proceeded to indicate that God had lied to her and Adam and that he was actually the one telling them the truth. He claimed that disregarding and disobeying God would bring them delight rather than death. He guaranteed that their enlightenment concerning evil would be enjoyable.

Jesus later described Satan in this manner: "He was a murderer from the beginning, and does not stand in the truth, because there is no truth in him. When he lies, he speaks out of his own character, for he is a liar and the father of lies." **John 8:44**

"So when the woman saw that the tree was good for food, and that it was a delight to the eyes, and that the tree was to be desired to make one wise, she took of its fruit and ate, and she also gave some to her husband who was with her, and he ate." **Genesis 3:6**

We haven't gotten three chapters into the Bible before we find the first people put on this planet failing to follow God's instructions; committing the first sin. Every human being who has lived on earth since that time, with the exception of Jesus Christ (God clothed in human flesh) has repeated the same sin scenario.

"None is righteous, no, not one; no one understands; no one seeks for God. All have turned aside; together they have become worthless; no one does good, not even one." **Romans 3:9-12**

The mission of Jesus Christ, Who the Bible tells us is both God's only Son (**John 3:16**) and God Himself (**John 10:30**), was to sacrifice Himself in order to pay the penalty required by mankind's sins (all of them). He was eligible to do this because He had no sin of His own (**2 Corinthians 5:21**).

Christ's redemptive mission began with a miracle, was continuously supported by miracles, and was confirmed as successfully completed by a miracle.

Christ coming to earth as our Savior Messiah was announced by God's prophet Isaiah seven hundred years before Christ's birth actually occurred.

"Therefore the Lord himself will give you a sign. Behold, the virgin shall conceive and bear a son, and shall call his name Immanuel." **Isaiah 7:14**

"For to us a child is born, to us a son is given, and the government will be on His shoulders. And He will be called Wonderful Counselor, Mighty God, Everlasting Father, Prince of Peace." **Isaiah 9:6**

The miraculous birth of Jesus via the virgin Mary, as prophesized by Isaiah, is what the world celebrates each year at Christmas.

"The angel said to her, 'Do not be afraid, Mary, for you have found favor with God. And behold, you will conceive in your womb and bear a son, and you shall call His name Jesus. He will be great and will be called the Son of the Most High. And the Lord God will give to Him the throne of his father David, and He will reign over the house of Jacob forever, and of His kingdom there will be no end.' And Mary said to the angel, 'How will this be, since I am a virgin?' And the angel answered her, 'The Holy Spirit will come upon you, and the power of the Most High will overshadow you; therefore the child to be born will be called holy—the Son of God.'" **Luke 1:30-35**

The earthly ministry of Jesus was also filled with physical and spiritual miracles that verified Who He was and what He came to earth to accomplish. Jesus said to the crowds of people that His miracles drew: "Believe me that I am in the Father and the Father is in Me, or else believe on account of the works themselves." **John 14:11**

The Prophet Isaiah stressed that fact that Christ's redemptive mission would result in His suffering and death (**Isaiah 53**) and we now know that is exactly what occurred. Death and the grave, however, could not hold our God-Savior captive.

After the crucifixion of Jesus Mary, Mary Magdalene and Salome had gone to anoint His body for burial. They were extremely surprised to find His tomb empty and even more surprised by the angel who sat on the grave stone by entrance to His tomb and said to them, "He is not here, for He has risen, as He said. Come, see the place where He lay." **Matthew 28:6**

The resurrection of Jesus Christ is the primary proof of the Christian faith. It is the truth that lies at the very foundation of the Gospel. Other doctrines of the Christian faith are important, but the resurrection is essential (**1 Corinthians 15:14**). Without a belief in the resurrection there can be no personal salvation.

The Bible says, "If you confess with your mouth that Jesus is Lord (the leader of your life) and believe in your heart that God raised Him from the dead, you will be saved (saved from the penalty of your sin)." **Romans 10:8, 9**

The Apostle Paul declared the victory over sin and Satan that was accomplished by Christ's death and resurrection.

"First of all, I taught you what I had received. It was this: Christ died for our sins as the Holy Writings said He would. Christ was buried. He was raised from the dead three days later as the Holy Writings said He would. Christ was seen by Peter. After that, the twelve followers saw Him. After that, more than 500 of His followers saw Him at one time. Most of them are still here, but some have died. After that, James saw Christ. Then all the missionaries saw Him. Last of all, Christ showed Himself to me." **1 Corinthians 15:3-8**

God now offers forgiveness of sin, restored spiritual life, and restored relationship with Himself as a grace gift to anyone willing by faith to believe and receive Jesus Christ as their Savior and the Lord of their life.

"God demonstrates His own love for us in this: While we were still sinners, Christ died for us." **Romans 5:8**

"For the wages of sin is death, but the gift of God is eternal life in Christ Jesus our Lord." **Romans 6:23**

"It is by grace you have been saved, through faith—and this is not from yourselves, it is the gift of God— not by works, so that no one can boast." **Ephesians 2:8-9**

In my book titled "Christ's Discipleship Deal," I discuss how receiving Jesus as your Savior and Lord requires becoming one of His followers; His devoted disciple. In order for this to occur you must be willing to repent of you sin and subsequently carry the cross of sacrificial Kingdom of God service that Jesus assigns each of His followers. "He said to all, 'If anyone would come after me, let him deny himself and take up his cross daily and follow me.'" Luke 9:23

Accepting the terms of Christ's discipleship deal establishes a covenant relationship between followers of Christ and God that comes with both benefits and responsibilities.

My second book, "What Do You Say to a Happy Heathen" describes how I first became a follower of Jesus Christ and what took place in the years that followed that decision.

Receiving Christ as your Savior has many present and future benefits which include forgiveness of all your sin along with restored eternal relationship with God and His family as saved citizens of the Kingdom of God. There are however, costs that must be considered (Luke 14:28). Jesus came to earth to save followers; not accumulate fans, entertain spectators, or cater to Christian consumers.

Being saved from the penalty of sin and slavery to Satan, is in many ways similar to what occurred in God delivering the Israelites from slavery in Egypt. They were saved from Pharaoh to live and labor as the people of God; to adopt the agenda and aims of God. God's purpose was for them to possess their land of promise rather than to be enslaved by Pharaoh and Egypt.

"When you were slaves of sin, you were free in regard to righteousness. But what fruit were you getting at that time from the things of which you are now ashamed? For the end of those things is death. But now that you have been set free from sin and have become slaves of God, the fruit you get leads to sanctification and its end, eternal life." **Romans 6:20-22**

Spiritual rebirth marks the beginning of our Jesus journey to our promise land. As the Hebrews followed God's cloud by day and fiery pillar by night toward their promise land so twenty-first century Christians are to follow the leadership of God's Holy Spirit Who Jesus sent to be our Helper, Counselor, and Guide.

"But the Helper, the Holy Spirit, whom the Father will send in My name, He will teach you all things and bring to your remembrance all that I have said to you." **John 14:26**

"When the Spirit of truth comes, He will guide you into all the truth." **John 16:13**

Functional Faith

Just prior to His exit from Earth, Jesus spoke with His first followers about the redemptive mission He had enlisted, prepared, and commissioned them to carry out as His Kingdom of God representatives; as the Messiah's missionaries.

"Then He opened their minds to understand the Scriptures, and said to them, 'Thus it is written, that the Christ should suffer and on the third day rise from the dead, and that repentance for the forgiveness of sins should be proclaimed in His name to all nations, beginning from Jerusalem. You are witnesses of these things. And behold, I am sending the promise of My Father upon you. But stay in the city until you are clothed with power from on high.'" **Luke 24:44-49**

Christ was clear concerning what His followers would be able to accomplish without His help.

"Abide in Me, and I in you. As the branch cannot bear fruit by itself, unless it abides in the vine, neither can you, unless you abide in Me. I am the vine; you are the branches. Whoever abides in Me and I in him, he it is that bears much fruit, for apart from Me you can do nothing." **John 15:4, 5**

I interpret what Jesus said as, "Without Me, your best is a bust!"

Faithfully following His instructions, which is always a great game plan, the startup team for the Jerusalem church plant waited for Christ's promised provision of power to arrive.

"When the day of Pentecost arrived, they were all together in one place. And suddenly there came from heaven a sound like a mighty rushing wind, and it filled the entire house where they were sitting. And divided tongues as of fire appeared to them and rested on each one of them. And they were all filled with the Holy Spirit and began to speak in other tongues as the Spirit gave them utterance. Now there were dwelling in Jerusalem Jews, devout men from every nation under heaven. And at this sound the multitude came together, and they were bewildered, because each one was hearing them speak in his own language." **Acts 2:1-6**

God's mission plan for the Jerusalem church was to fill every follower of Christ with Holy Spirit power and then send them out into their area of primary mission responsibility to proclaim the Gospel. These missionaries were all given the special ability by the Holy Spirit to proclaim the Gospel in languages they had never learned. This strategy proved to be extremely effective.

"There were added that day about three thousand souls." **Acts 2:41**

God knew that the Hebrews were not going to be able to take possession of their promise land without His help. Throughout their time and travels in the desert He was trying to teach them how to carry out the work and warfare involved in taking possession of their promise land by faith. All of what happened to them was intended to convince them not to rely upon their own resourcefulness but rather increase their trust and dependency on Him.

The Israelites were required, in partnership with God, to proactively perform the work and warfare required to take possession of their promise land. Jesus commissioned His church and sent us out to take possession of our promise lands with words that sound, at least to me, much like what God said to Joshua (**Joshua 1:3-9**).

"Jesus came and said to them, 'All authority in heaven and on earth has been given to Me. Go therefore and make disciples of all nations, baptizing them in the name of the Father and of the Son and of the Holy Spirit, teaching them to observe all that I have commanded you. And behold, I am with you always, to the end of the age.'" **Matthew 28:18-20**

"You will receive power when the Holy Spirit has come upon you, and you will be My witnesses in Jerusalem and in all Judea and Samaria, and to the end of the earth." **Acts 1:8**

Please notice that in order for what Christ's spoke to His church about to actually occur, His followers must:

- be proactive and strategic in our redemptive mission work; in possessing our promise land
- go to those who don't know Christ rather than waiting for them to come to church
- attempt to reach everyone with God's Gospel of grace; no settling for "only a few will do"
- make sure our mission remains primarily, proactively redemptive
- rely by faith upon Christ's partnership and provision for whatever is required to accomplish His primary purpose; seeking and saving the lost
- determine to function as a spiritual hospital seeking to save as many of the living as possible rather than a hospice making the dying more comfortable

The Exodus journey of the Israelites from captivity in Egypt to Canaan was entirely about God attempting to prepare His people to take possession of their promise land by faith; by putting into practice the promises they had been provided and the principles they had learned. The same is true for every twenty-first follower of Christ and every local church.

The Apostle Paul stresses the importance of faith for followers of Christ when he writes under the inspiration of the Holy Spirit: "I am not ashamed of the gospel, for it is the power of God for salvation to everyone who believes, to the Jew first and also to the Greek. For in it the righteousness of God is revealed from faith for faith, as it is written, 'The righteous shall live by faith.'" **Romans 1:16, 17**

Let me ask you; if you are sure you are saved, how did that happen? What was it that you were required to do in order to become a follower of Jesus Christ; believe and receive Him as Savior and Lord by faith!

"To all who did receive him, who believed in his name, he gave the right to become children of God, who were born, not of blood nor of the will of the flesh nor of the will of man, but of God." **John 1:12**

"For by grace you have been saved through faith. And this is not your own doing; it is the gift of God, not a result of works, so that no one may boast." **Ephesians 2:8, 9**

Every born again believer was saved by faith. We believed what we heard or read was true, we relied upon fact that what God inspired to be written in the Scriptures was trustworthy.

Listen to what the Apostle Paul wrote about the importance of what we believe actually being true: "If Christ hasn't been raised from the dead, our preaching is useless and so is our faith....your faith is futile and you are still in your sins." **1 Corinthians 15:14, 17**

We have all been saved out of captivity to Satan and sin by faith. We have also been set free to serve God by faith. It is just as foolish to believe we can claim our intended promise land by our own best effort as it is to believe we can save ourselves from the penalty of sin.

Paul called the Galatian Christians foolish because after being saved by faith they were attempting to live, and labor according to the Old Covenant religious works plan.

"O foolish Galatians! Who has bewitched you? It was before your eyes that Jesus Christ was publicly portrayed as crucified. Let me ask you only this: Did you receive the Spirit by works of the law or by hearing with faith? Are you so foolish? Having begun by the Spirit, are you now being perfected by the flesh? Did you suffer so many things in vain—if indeed it was in vain? Does He who supplies the Spirit to you and works miracles among you do so by works of the law, or by hearing with faith— just as Abraham believed God, and it was counted to him as righteousness? Know then that it is those of faith who are the sons of Abraham. And the Scripture, foreseeing that God would justify the Gentiles by faith, preached the gospel beforehand to Abraham, saying, 'In you shall all the nations be blessed.' So then, those who are of faith are blessed along with Abraham, the man of faith. For all who rely on works of the law are under a curse; for it is written, 'Cursed be everyone who does not abide by all things written in the Book of the Law, and do them.' Now it is evident that no one is justified before God by the law, for 'The righteous shall live by faith.'" **Galatians 3:1-11**

It is essential that the righteous, those who go about following Christ according to His plan rather than coming up with our own plan, learn how to carry out our kingdom work and warfare in the right manner; by faith!

This means that the priority task of every local church must be training the members of our congregation, Christ's faithful followers, to achieve spiritual maturity and accomplish the Kingdom of God ministry and mission that we have each been enlisted, equipped, and entrusted by the Holy Spirit to perform, by faith.

I believe that local churches have been commissioned by Christ to perform three primary functions related to the life, and labor of our members.

Function 1 Facilitate connectedness between God and His family, through teaching, worship, prayer, and fellowship. This is our maturity function.

Function 2 Properly prepare (train) Christ's followers, in partnership with the Holy Spirit, to fit and function together as the body of Christ. This is our ministry function.

Function 3 Enlist and equip Christ's followers to proactively share the grace and Gospel of Jesus Christ with those within their primary spheres of influence, and throughout the world. Empowered and led by the Holy Spirit, we engage in the work and warfare required to fully possess our promise land(s) by faith. This is our mission function.

Every other task the local church performs should be accomplished in support of these three primary functions.

The Promise Land Principle
CHAPTER 11

Claiming Your Promise Land

The Holy Spirit laid two primary concerns upon my heart that motivated me to write this book.

Concern 1   I encounter far too many followers of Jesus Christ wandering around in some wilderness, grumbling and complaining about their circumstances; enduring their enslavement rather than enjoying life in their promise land. My concern is that many of Christ's followers will die in the wilderness without ever entering, much less fully possessing their promise land.

Concern 2   I encounter far too many local churches whose members spend the majority of their time wandering around their own property rather than performing the work and warfare, in partnership with the Holy Spirit, required to take full possession of their primary area of mission responsibility; their promise land. Believers who have become content with sitting on the premises rather than standing on the promises.

As we each prayerfully and carefully consider individually and corporately where our promise lands are and what might be involved in taking possession of them, let us reflect upon the terms and conditions of God's promised provision.

"If you are willing and obedient, you shall eat the good of the land." **Isaiah 1:19**

1   In order to claim your promise land, you must first conquer the opposition and clear the obstacles standing in your way

In His book "The Purpose of Temptation," Bob Mumford introduces, "The Law of the Four Ps." God gives us a Promise, which is linked to a Principle (in this case the Promise Land Principle), followed by a Problem (the opposition and obstacles that the Israelites encountered), leading to a Provision.

The purpose of the problems God either plans or permits, is to teach us how to depend upon Him; how to partner with Him by faith in overcoming our obstacles and opposition. The first thing that should come to mind when we encounter seas that need to part, or walls that need to fall is, "I/we can't, but God can."

2   In order to claim your promise land, you must meet all of God's terms and conditions

God is completely dependable and reliable. If we meet His terms and conditions the outcome He promises to provide is guaranteed. If we fail to follow His instructions, for any reason, even what we believe at the time to be a good reason, failure is a certainty. God's provision never comes until we make the decision to total trust and uncompromisingly obey Him by faith; and then follow through with what we have committed to do.

God guaranteed great things to the Israelites even before they entered their promise land. If they would diligently obey Him and if they were "careful to do everything He instructed/commanded them to do," He promised prosperity and protection, favor and health, abundance and peace, victory and success, and freedom from fear. But many of His promises came with conditions: If they failed to observe His instructions/commandments they would experience certain defeat and failure. They would wander in wildernesses groping for direction as a blind man gropes in the darkness (**Deuteronomy 28:29**).

I want us to examine one of God's conditional promises that has a major impact upon our endeavors to take possession of our twenty-first century promise lands.

After a botched ministry attempt to deliver a demon possessed young boy, Christ's first followers came to Him with questions concerning the reasons for their failure.

"Then the disciples came to Jesus privately and said, 'Why could we not cast it out?' He said to them, 'Because of your little faith. For truly, I say to you, if you have faith like a grain of mustard seed, you will say to this mountain, Move from here to there, and it will move, and nothing will be impossible for you.'" **Matthew 17:19, 20**

His followers had failed to meet some condition required by faith! Their faith was inadequate to overcome the opposition's entrenchment within the young boy. They needed to develop greater faith in order to possess that particular promise land.

So how do twenty-first followers of Jesus go about developing the faith we require to overcome the opposition and obstacles we encounter?

Romans 12:3 tells us that God has given each of Christ's servants a measure of faith. Your faith grows according to what you do with it. Christ's story concerning the resources entrusted to three employees by a business owner illustrates this truth (**Matthew 25:14-30**). Two of the employees used what that had been allocated profitably while the third did not. The two profitable employees who wisely invested what they had been given were praised and their resources were increased. The third employee, who offered his employer excuses rather than earnings, was penalized.

Jesus concluded His parable by making a point about what we are intended to do with whatever God entrusts to us; especially our opportunities and measure of faith.

"For to everyone who has will more be given, and he will have an abundance. But from the one who has not, even what he has will be taken away." **Matthew 25:29**

Far too many believers and local churches are doing what the foolish fellow in Christ's parable did. They bury their faith while claiming to be conservative and cautious. They aren't properly using what God has given them to accomplish what matters most; seeking to bring God's salvation to the lost who live within their primary area of mission responsibility. If you want your faith to profitably grow, you've got to properly plant it. Faith demands risk, challenge, and change! Only faith results in God's intended reward. According to **Hebrews 11:6**, only faith pleases God.

Your faith grows as you partner with the Holy Spirit and experience His miraculous power, protection, and provision. Your measure of faith grows, like the muscles of your body, when you properly put it into practice. Paul was describing the faith that God progressively developed in him through his missionary exploits when he wrote: "I can do all things through Him who strengthens me." **Philippians 4:13**

By faith, Paul was confident he could do whatever needed to be done to accomplish God's purpose and plans. He had learned through personal experience that the God with Whom all things are possible (**Matthew 19:26**), was continually at work in him and through him, amidst all his constantly changing circumstances.

3   In order to claim and conquer your promise land, your faith must become Bible based

Faith is the expression of a Bible based belief (promise or principle), or some specific instruction received from the Holy Spirit. To take appropriate action based upon faith, followers of Christ must receive specific, clearly understood, and confidently undertaken instructions from God.

"Faith comes from hearing the message, and the message is heard through the word about Christ." **Romans 10:17**

The Bible is intended to be God's faith based instruction book that contains the promises and principles God wants every believer to learn and live; to read and heed.

"All Scripture is God-breathed and is useful for teaching, rebuking, correcting and training in righteousness, so that the servant of God may be thoroughly equipped for every good work." **2 Timothy 3:16, 17**

The Bible wasn't inspired by God merely to provide information for us to acquire but instructions for us to act upon and commands for us to comply with by faith.

James makes this point compellingly clear.

"What good is it, my brothers, if someone says he has faith but does not have works?..... Faith by itself, if it does not have works, is dead......But someone will say, 'You have faith and I have works.' Show me your faith apart from your works, and I will show you my faith by my works.....Do you want to be shown, you foolish person, that faith apart from works is useless? Was not Abraham our father justified by works when he offered up his son Isaac on the altar? You see that faith was active along with his works, and faith was completed by his works; and the Scripture was fulfilled that says, 'Abraham believed God, and it was counted to him as righteousness — and he was called a friend of God.' As the body apart from the spirit is dead, so also faith apart from works is dead." **James 2:14, 17, 18, 20-23, 26.**

"Be doers of the word, and not hearers only, deceiving yourselves." **James 1:22**

Abraham's life and labor as a servant of God, like ours, was a mixture of faith and foolishness. His faith, however, finally grew to the size whereby he was willing to do whatever God instructed him to do; including sacrificing the son God had promised to provide for him.

"After these things (after all the other things that had taken place involving Abraham and Sarah coming to their promise land in Canaan) God tested

Abraham and said to him, 'Abraham!' And he said, 'Here I am.' He said, 'Take your son, your only son Isaac, whom you love, and go to the land of Moriah, and offer him there as a burnt offering on one of the mountains of which I shall tell you.'" **Genesis 22:1-2**

Those of us who study Scripture realize that God did not actually require Abraham to sacrifice his son. The point I want to make sure you see is that the promise land principle was operative in Abraham's partnership with the Lord, just exactly as it operated throughout the Exodus story and continues to operate in our partnership with the Holy Spirit today.

Let me bring this book to a close by summarizing for you "The Promise Land Principle" as I believe it applies to contemporary Christians, local churches, and Christian organizations.

The Promise Land Principle

- God sets captive people free from the power and prison of sin to participate in Christ's redemptive mission by individually and corporately taking possession of their designated promise lands.
- God allows, or creates circumstances designed to prepare the faith that followers of Christ require to possess our promise land(s).
- God then offers us the opportunity, through our work and warfare accomplished in partnership with the Holy Spirit, to possess our promise land(s).
- Christ's followers must be faithful in complying with God's commands and following His instructions regardless of our circumstances or consequences.
- Whether we end up wandering in some wilderness or prospering in our promise land depends entirely upon our belief-based, faith choices.

I am convinced that God has a promised land planned for each follower of Christ that can only be experienced through consistently and completely carrying out the terms of the covenant He has individually and corporately established with us.

Carpe diem! God's best for you and me is yet to be.

Printed in the United States
by Baker & Taylor

Printed in the United States
By Bookmasters